Little Mitchie

LET'S LOOK INSIDE A FIRE TRUCK

LET'S LOOK INSIDE: VEHICLES

PAUL ZACHARY

CREATING YOUNG NONFICTION READERS

Little Mitchie books spark curiosity and support early nonfiction reading for students in Grades 2-3. Designed to build vocabulary, support second language learners, and prepare readers for middle-grade content, each book includes helpful tips for parents and educators to build confidence and deepen understanding of the world.

TIPS FOR READING NONFICTION WITH BEGINNING READERS

Talk about Nonfiction

Begin by explaining that nonfiction books give us information that is true. The book will be organized around a specific topic or idea, and we may learn new facts through reading.

Look at the Parts

Most nonfiction books have helpful features. Our *Little Mitchie* titles include color photographs and graphic aids, a table of contents, a glossary, and an index. Share the purpose of these features with your reader.

Color Photos and Graphic Aids

A lot of information can be found by "reading" photos, charts, maps, and other graphic aids found within nonfiction texts. Help your reader learn more about the different ways information can be displayed.

Table of Contents

Located at the front of the book, this list shows the big ideas within the text and the page numbers where they can be found.

Glossary

Located at the back of the book, the glossary defines key words and phrases that are related to the topic. These words and phrases can be found in the text in colored type.

Index

Located at the back of the book, an index is an alphabetical list of topics and the page numbers where they can be found.

With a little help and guidance about reading nonfiction, you can feel good about introducing a young reader to the world of *Little Mitchie* nonfiction books.

Little Mitchie is an imprint of:

Mitchell Lane
PUBLISHERS

2001 SW 31st Avenue
Hallandale, FL 33009
mitchelllanepub.com

First Edition, 2027.

Author: Paul Zachary
Designer: Rhea Magaro
Editor: Tricia Hoffman

Library of Congress Cataloging-in-Publication Data
Title: Let's Look Inside a Fire Truck / by Paul Zachary.

Description: Hallandale, FL :
Mitchell Lane Publishers, [2027]

Identifiers:
ISBN 979-8-89260-882-4 (library bound)
ISBN 979-8-90145-048-2 (paperback)
ISBN 979-8-89260-985-2 (eBook)

Library of Congress Control Number: 2026930134

Photo credits: Alamy: Mel Stoutsenberger, 10; dov makabaw, 13; Hrishchenko, 14; Shutterstock: Le Do, 1; Le Do, 3; Michael Derrer Fuchs, 5; dotshock, 6; EdBelkin, 9; MATTHEW GOLDBERG, 12; Oleksandr Lumppini, 16; sonya etchison, 18; Ivelin Denev, 21; Tyler Olson, 22

TABLE OF CONTENTS

Chapter One
RACING TO THE RESCUE! . . . 4

Chapter Two
GEAR AND EQUIPMENT. . . 8

Chapter Three
TOOLS FOR EVERY JOB . . . 15

Chapter Four
READY FOR ACTION . . . 19

A LOOK INSIDE 22
GLOSSARY . . . 23
FURTHER READING . . . 24
ON THE INTERNET . . . 24
INDEX . . . 24

Chapter One

RACING TO THE RESCUE!

A bright red fire truck speeds down the street. Its lights flash. Its **siren** wails. Cars move to the side of the road so the truck can pass.

Have you ever wondered what's inside a fire truck? Let's take a look!

FIRE FACT

Not all fire trucks are red. Some are yellow, white, or lime green.

A fire truck is like a giant **toolbox** on wheels. It carries everything **firefighters** need to rescue people and stay safe.

At the front of the truck is the cab. This is where the firefighters sit while traveling to an **emergency**. They buckle their seat belts and wear headsets to hear directions from the station.

Chapter Two

GEAR AND EQUIPMENT

Firefighters keep their heavy coats, helmets, gloves, and boots behind the cab. Their special clothing protects them from heat and smoke. Some of their gear is **fire-resistant**. Other gear helps them breathe clean air inside burning buildings.

There are many hoses! Some hoses are short and thick. Others are long and thin.

Firefighters connect hoses to fire **hydrants** to get water. They spray the water to put out fires. A **nozzle** at the end of the hose controls how fast the water comes out.

A ladder truck has a long, metal ladder that can stretch as tall as a building. Firefighters use it to reach high windows or roofs. Some ladders have a basket at the top to carry people to safety.

FIRE FACT

There are many different kinds of fire trucks. Pumper trucks spray water. Ladder trucks reach high places. Rescue trucks carry special tools.

FiRE FACT

Fire trucks are checked every day to make sure all the equipment works properly.

Chapter Three

TOOLS FOR EVERY JOB

There are many tools inside the truck. Firefighters use axes to break doors and saws to cut wood. Crowbars pry things open. Flashlights help them see in dark places. Radios help them call for backup. The truck may also carry **first-aid** supplies and oxygen tanks.

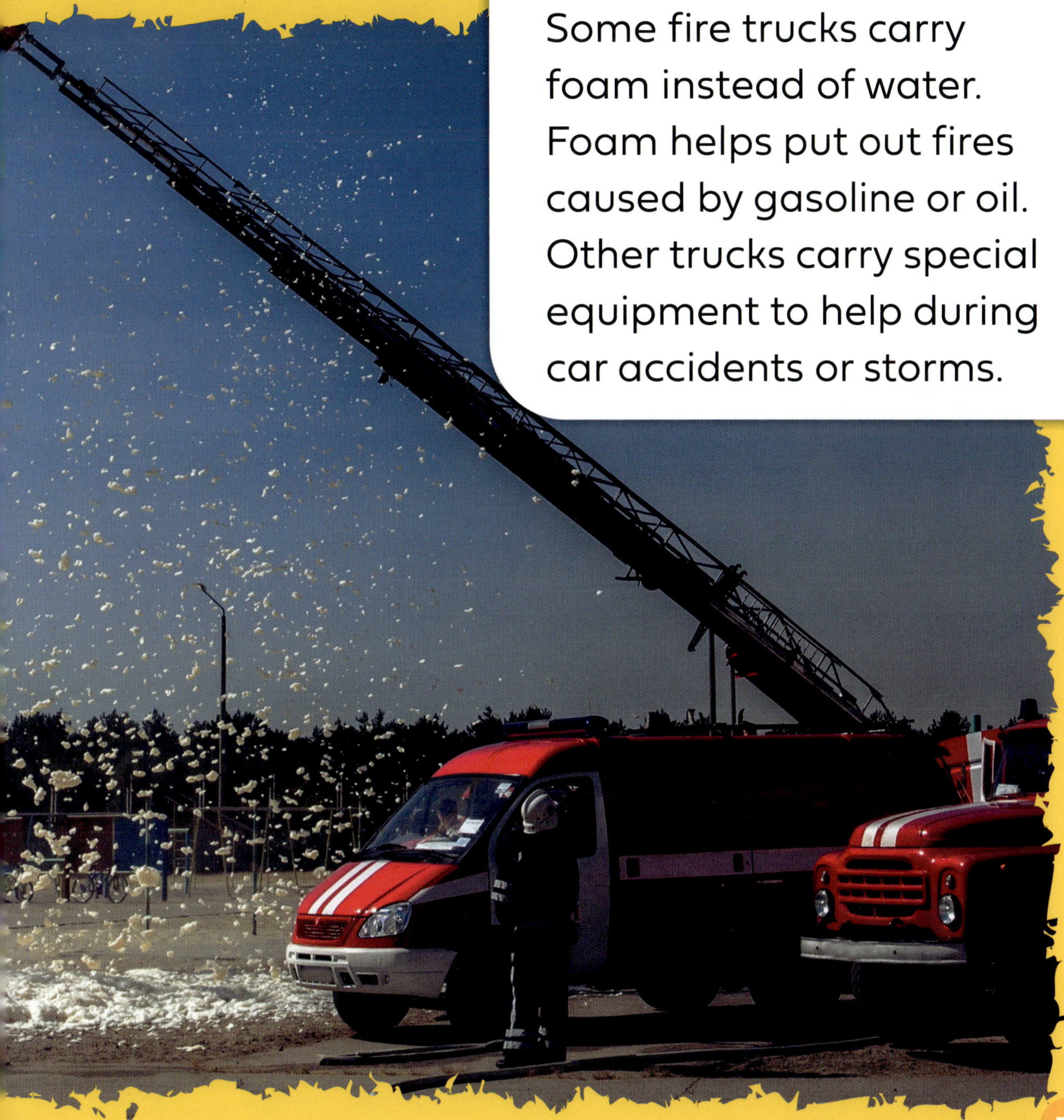

Some fire trucks carry foam instead of water. Foam helps put out fires caused by gasoline or oil. Other trucks carry special equipment to help during car accidents or storms.

Chapter Four

READY FOR ACTION

A fire truck may look simple from the outside, but inside it is full of life-saving tools. Every part has a purpose. Each tool helps firefighters protect people, pets, and homes.

The next time you see a fire truck, imagine all the amazing things riding along inside!

FIRE FACT

Visiting a fire station is a great way to learn more!

A LOOK INSIDE

A. CAB
B. LADDER
C. HOSE
D. LIGHTS

GLOSSARY

emergency (i-mur-juhn-see) a sudden problem or danger that needs help right away

firefighter (fire-fye-tur) a person who is trained to put out fires and keeps people safe

fire-resistant (fire-ri-zis-tuhnt) fabric that can resist fire for a short amount of time

first-aid (furst-ayd) basic medical help given to someone who is hurt before a doctor arrives

hydrant (hye-druhnt) a large pipe in the street that supplies water to use against fires

nozzle (nah-zuhl) the tip of a hose that controls how water sprays out

siren (sye-ruhn) a loud warning sound used on emergency vehicles

toolbox (tool-bahks) a box designed for storing or carrying hand tools

FURTHER READING

Amoroso, Cynthia. *Fire Trucks.* The Child's World, 2023.

Deniston, Natalie. *Fire Trucks.* Tadpole Books, 2025.

ON THE INTERNET

Fire Engine Facts for Kids

https://kids.kiddle.co/Fire_engine?

A simple encyclopedia-style page with easy-to-understand facts about fire trucks and how they help firefighters.

Explore a Truck

https://sparky.org/firetrucks

A fun kid-oriented site from the National Fire Protection Association with facts, games, and activities about fire trucks and how they help firefighters.

INDEX

cab 7, 8, 22
clothing 8
equipment 8, 17
foam 17
hose 10
ladder 12, 13, 22
nozzle 10
tools 13, 15, 19